Rumors of Separate Worlds

Rumors of

POEMS BY

ROBERT COLES

Separate Worlds

UNIVERSITY OF IOWA PRESS

IOWA CITY

University of Iowa Press, Iowa City 52242

Library of Congress
Cataloging-in-Publication Data

Coles, Robert.
  Rumors of separate worlds: poems/by
Robert Coles.—1st ed.
    p.   cm.
  ISBN 0-87745-258-X, ISBN 0-87745-260-1
(pbk.)
  I. Title.
PS3553.O47456R8   1989   89-32838
811'.54—dc20   CIP

In grateful memory of W.C.W.—for

helping a life get started.

To J.H.C.—with love and with thanks for

those thirty years.

CONTENTS

On the Day Jesus Christ Was Born

INTRODUCTION

These poems began in my medical school days, when great good fortune gave me visit after visit with William Carlos Williams, sometimes at his home, sometimes as he made visits to his patients. He was getting old, and he could, I noticed, suddenly turn cranky as well as tired—an occasion, often, for a shrewd, sardonic comment about a person or a place. Not rarely, he made himself the butt of his remark, a propensity he had shown, I knew, in *Paterson*—an almost Augustinian self-scrutiny, lest he himself disregard one of his central points: that words and ideas can be all too cheap, the big challenge being our willingness to match them with everyday conduct. At other times the wonderfully knowing doctor and poet became a soft-spoken, reflective man who was nearing the end of his life and had some memories to share, some thoughts to speak. I remember them well, a mind's return to its past, and a mind's continuing interest in sizing things up, rendering to another what is felt, believed. Almost always, I eventually realized, and unsurprisingly, this poet thought as poets do, and, often enough, his talk resembled his written words—the condensations, the suggestive or provocative use of language, the images and symbols and metaphors. We were having a conversation, but I was hearing a kind of poetry.

Over the years I've not wanted to forget Dr. Williams, and under various circumstances I've often tried to think of what he might think, were he now here with me. Lord, I'll never be able to talk or write as he could, but a mentor's student has a right to follow suit in his own limited, halting way—hence my habit, from time to time, of doing what he once recommended I do when I began my work in the South, studying school desegregation, three or four years before his death: "Pay attention to the music you hear in those kids as they talk. Write down the lines they speak as they speak them. Pull it all together in different ways, not only in medical reports or essays. Try capturing the images, the rhythm, the tilt of the talk, the drift, the ups and downs." I wasn't completely sure, as I heard him giving me that advice, what I was to do, if I was to measure up to his suggestion, but I did try, and I know I followed his advice, given me many times, that I not "push too hard on theory." How much alive he still is in my mind, and in my teaching life, as I try to introduce him to others!

I'm not yet as old as Dr. Williams was when I first got to know him, but I'm getting there. I can't give voice to the world's sights and sounds as he did, but I still remember his suggestions, his (at times) strenuous urging. Here I respond to him, to his giant influence on me—on so many of us in America—in three ways: with an effort to remember scenes in my own life; with an effort to convey some of what my work here and abroad has offered me, prompted in me; and, finally, with an effort to call upon many Christmas days, spent all over the place—a mind's struggle to make sense of apparently limitless ironies, ambiguities, contradictions, not to mention fatefulness, the rule of luck, the reign of the arbitrary and the accidental in our lives. Thank you, yet once more, and still, Dr. William Carlos Williams, and thank you, Jane, who gave me the strength, day after day, to keep taking the chances, to follow as best I could the New Jersey doctor's lead.

Christmas, 1988

And the air lying over the water
lifts the ripples, brother
to brother, touching as the mind touches,
counter-current, upstream
brings in the fields, hot and cold
parallel but never mingling, one that whirls
backward at the brink and curls invisibly
upward, fills the hollow, whirling,
an accompaniment—but apart, observant of
the distress, sweeps down or up clearing
the spray—

        brings in the rumors of separate
worlds, the birds as against the fish, the grape
to the green weed that streams out undulant
with the current at low tide beside the
bramble in blossom, the storm by the flood—
song and wings—

      —William Carlos Williams
      Paterson, Book I, Section II

Remembering a World

MOTHER'S TOLSTOY

To S.Y.C.
1905–1985

She first met Anna in Iowa,
A farmer's granddaughter,
Comfortable in fading moonlight,
Head leaning on cows,
Balancing milk-pails,
Waiting for a chance,
The sun fully in charge of the crops,
To visit another farm;
To overhear Levin overhearing himself,
See Vronsky riding a horse to the ground,
Cringe at the official husband's
Visit from the city:
They are all alike
In the thick glass of their eyes,
The wiring that short-circuits all voices,
Save their ukases for this or that tsar.
Anna came to her in special places:
On the swing her older brother built
Before he left to win women,
Fight for America "over there";
In the attic, where she could look
With the camera's help
At the plains beauty of an aunt
Inviting speculations from posterity.
And when, finally, Anna went to meet the train
She did, too—heard the high screech from Chicago
Coming toward the river yards,

Wondered about life as people do
Letting go.

In her hospital bed in Boston
Anna was at her side,
Even when visiting hours were over;
And others—Prince Nekhlyudov,
Whom she'd met many times
In a life's travel toward that room,
Where she was preparing,
As the prince did, for the Meeting.
Just before it she read again of
The lawyer Ilych's last moment with his servant,
Of a "master" and his servant—all those servants,
Going back to Him who served us all.

She was going back herself,
And had begun traveling preparations
During a high school summer,
When she enlisted Tolstoy's help
In her search for peace.
When the politicians shouted "no more war,"
And her brother's dead body came to mind,
She raged, until the book taught her
Others were there, waiting to console:
The losers, called winners—
And so it goes, Tolstoy knew
When young, and never forgot,
Even in that railroad station
Where he might have seen Anna
As his own train pulled in.

The last words were a soft good-bye,
No tear visible to a trained surveyor
Of this century's well-trod Berggasse.
The right hand exercised its last authority,
Reached for Tolstoy's hands,
And, touching him, returned to her side
So that she could smile and leave;
So that the son and grandson could
Move up their own date of departure,
Pick up Tolstoy's harvest,
Carry it home to the kitchen,
Where with bread and wine it belongs.

DAD'S WALKS WITH ORWELL

To P.C.
1900–1985

The town's streets were always sending him
Invitations he never declined;
"Up and at 'em," he'd tell me,
The fierce warrior's phrase a feint.
He had peace in mind
I would realize as we took to talking
While walking, and always the pointing:
Here it goes like this,
There it's another story—
And he had the words for it.
A Yorkshire youth spent
Walking fast—a sport across the sea
Long before joggers added
Their struggle to the world's supply.

He came to the States for science' sake,
To a place proud to be known
Only by three letters—
Where intellect's might had been asked
To marry technology;
But he had been to Suffolk
On walking marathons,
Waded in the Orwell river
Before it had found its
Immortality in a mere man,
Who knew how to keep his eyes open
While moving from capital to capital,
While daring the deep crawl with miners,
While mourning the murder of Spain's democracy.

When we crossed our little river
On Boston's border,
Dad's index finger did its dance,
Whirled through the murky fall air,
Clearing things up—and such a spring to his step.
I groaned, wanted to slow down;
But no, time was running out,
He knew, then, smack in the middle
Of what later would be called
The "low, dishonest decade."

Homeward he'd always recapitulate:
The first surrender to neighborhoods,
Followed by the second summary action,
And then the man, and his books—
George, by the river they shared.
Two Englishmen in my mind
Who wandered and wondered,
Who were weary of cant,
Wary of all the hustlers on all the sidewalks,
But loved looking, listening.
We could always count on tea and scones
And another scene to lamp—
While a coughing Orwell,
His bed a tower,
Saw blinds coming down everywhere.

MISS AVERY'S CLASS

Memories not of madrilène,
But of pictures of presidents,
A teacher's odd green ink,
The flag hanging impassive
Before arms stretched with daily reverence,
The maps rich with real estate—
Traps for all those tests.
"I'm a Green Mountain girl,"
Her head tossing back white hair.
Our eyes claimed the words of books,
But we heard her pacing,
Walking those aisles:
A long Vermont leader rope—
Lest we stray.
Lincoln's resurrection
Took place in her history class;
We wondered why she became wet staring,
Gave us his heavy eyes in hers—
Lucky for her and us
The ignorance of an age
Yet to stoop to psychology.
One day she told us—
Even though it was the fifth grade
And now I'm in my fifth decade
I can hear the words,
The north wind picking us up,
Carrying us where (she must have hoped)
We'd stay forever:
"Washington was the father,
He the son, who died
For us to be free, you and me."

Our heads fell;
With chalk in hand
She called the Bible to the blackboard;
We followed suit—
My father's black pen, black ink
Witnesses to the message.
At home mother said an excited yes.
We never stopped to think
The Republic was in jeopardy
While we prayed in school.

NEW JERSEY BOYS
To W.C.W.

You two gardeners,
Both you bards, Bruce and Bill,
The Boss and the Doc,
Who never wanted to skip
The heartbeat of home—
Stay there, your choice:
Claiming the spread below the Hudson.
No bridge or tunnel worked for you,
The local turf gave you plenty to do—
Soil to pick up with bare hands;
Bring sun to warm it up,
Let drafts of air turn it on,
See its excitement grow.
Let the twin tallest buildings in the world
Signal their dough to the torch-lady nearby;
Lots of folks who scare up the blinds in the morning
Are spared the hangout—the hangups—of the big shots.

You two gardeners and your trips to the city:
"The Lonely Street" was followed
Decades later by "Racing in the Streets."
Each of you made the trek:
So many hustles to see,
All the colors and sounds, the words and deals,
Cards to be dealt, decks stacked,
A throw of the dice daily:
Plain life and crying shame deaths,
None of the Eros and Thanatos stuff
You hear in abstract elsewheres.
"Hey," you both pleaded,
"No starch in the shirts."

Both you gardeners raked:
Sweat all day and kiss
When you're lucky to find the lips.
No tax credits, just the tax itself, all the time,
Hoping for a break, a day off
Now and then, and the kids, they might do better,
Though it's always tough in Paterson,
And lots of times Nebraska is no picnic.

You guys, the gardener Walt's kin,
Whose beard we all know
(Its secrets keep a growth industry busy—
Leafing through his grass)
You two, from Ridge Road and E Street,
Each out to put it on the line, put them there:
Ordinary ones, whose lumps pollsters rush
To palpate only now and then.
You two are permanent guests,
Listening and showing your love in words, in notes
Two bards, Bruce and Bill,
The Boss and the Doc: America—
Love it or leave it to you both to know,
And give back to us, maybe our only chance.

LAST CLASS

There, waiting for their final glass of water,
The students sit watching the teacher sip,
Ready to walk the wire one more time
Before Christmas closes down the place.
Outside the hungry shoppers reach;
Here, in this room of human tides,
Ruled by the hour,
He offers *Middlemarch*, the last meal.
Then, those farewell poems to read.
By now we've heard of them,
His friend Ed Sissman singing—
The urgent call to Orwell.
Next, a grave salute to the dead,
The young men who went to war,
Against their will found new homes,
Left names but no addresses,
No visitors to see—
Sharing with the Galilean those last three hours.
The Lord keeps visiting His Son, surely;
So do we ours through Spender's
Thinking of the "truly great."
Finally, the good-bye moment
Calls for the one who stayed
Long enough to see himself enter history—
After many years in the College of Hard Knocks.
Frost's "reluctance" was not for tears.
But he cried alone: never for presidents,
Nor when offered the honorary degrees
He held gladly and let go discreetly
With a velocity never measured.

The church bell speaks its demand,
We gather ourselves for the holiday
Season of many lives saying good-byes,
Hellos, the repetitions—
Like the course, they will also have their last turn.

THE ALMONER

To D.D.
1897–1980

Nearer to Jesus in time and place
The almoner did what we were
Told to do by the visitor
Sent with messages:
Conventual duties—
Bread for churning acid,
Cloth as another layer of skin.
Not by law,
Not for the economy's sake,
Not to pat those with arms cut off—
The triumph of a teasing exercise;
But in a hurry of obedience,
Mindful that generosity is not gentility,
Nor a ticket for upward mobility.
To give is to signal
The jeopardy of a soul in need.
Dorothy Day, offering bread, pleaded:
"I'm hungry, too."

THE SIGHT OF THE BOYS

To R.E.C.,
D.A.C.,
M.H.C.

Now is in the mind,
Since they have left their three rooms,
Leaving us room to remember
What was, what we once thought
Would always be,
What we now glimpse
While brushing teeth, climbing stairs—
The bodies crouched over the years,
Dangling over the planet,
The Voyagers they, too, are.
Smiling as if Lucifer had never fallen,
They can build with sand forever;
Playing with "jobbies," with words,
Breaking rules in their own kingdoms,
Collecting at go, laughing while in jail,
Buying the best places,
Millionaires before Megabucks
Ever came to remind us of what we lost;
Saying good morning like conquistadores,
Good night and believing it—
We, too, could then believe and sleep:
Draw our own pictures in the dark—
For a while not hedging hope.

GRADY AND ARAN

G., 1964–1979
A., 1979 –

Your eyes watched us every minute,
All those years;
Your electricity awakened all our circuits,
Wired the house
With currents of animated concern,
A compliment to humans,
But for you, living a life
Of attentive attachment,
Of knowing observation—
Dreams of growling glory,
Escapades beyond our knowing,
All surrendered for our sakes.
Most of all, the forgiveness—
Your hearts beating for us,
No sense of our sins:
What we forgot to remember,
Overlooked while looking inward
Or outward, but not at you.
Always your eyes remained ready,
Eager at the sight of our desires—
We poor masters,
Who do so need your love
To fill those full and busy lives.
Some heady ones say
"Transitional objects," teddy bears
Who help children's bridges—
Mom to the world at large.
You helped build us,
Gave us transition, as age moved in:
Always there to receive the leash,

Lead us from ourselves
To a kingdom of kindness
Whose boundaries we knew fully
Only when its rulers had taken leave of us.

The concept of class
Is understood by a hungry bird,
Who scans the steep, untouched snow
Before presenting its prettiness
To people on the inside of nature,
The berries unwiped from their breakfast faces
Looking always for more fulfillment.

SECOND NEW YORK INAUGURATION

Looking out at the Empire
The governor's three old ones dared not smile
Lest their luck run out—
Challenged by someone
Who has owned manners for a century or more.
Let *them* be all that they are
And no one lifts a brow,
But let one of us forget our face
For five seconds, and everyone says:
Dixie won't clap,
The prairie will forget its populist past,
Turn its back on a child of the Lady Liberty
Whom Mario prepares to address—
The words of a son
Who is an early riser,
Writes his diary as if a French curé
In a village confessional had whispered hints,
Writes his own speeches,
A stumping miracle,
Their nerve and muscle
Part of his powerful body politic,
His hands reaching to
Every color and collar,
A common prayer: all sorts and conditions,
Spoken to common folk,
Who want to be part of the family
He urges us all to join;
Who have had it with splits and losses,
Who will say yes
(A prayer to the future,
A prayer for the future)

When they see those O's,
Being tired of N's
(So are Washington, Jefferson, Lincoln, maybe
When they look down on Johnson, Nixon, Reagan),
And who will say bravo
For mother Immaculata, for the in-law Raffas.
They sat rapt in loving, poised attention,
Remembering the grocer, his slow climb,
His day and night grip on the ladder:
It is his Mario, many of us hope,
Who will someday enter Casa Blanca,
An important new chapter in our nation's story.

ON DUTCH'S DEATH
In memory of A.O.L.

The doctor's face on a December day—
Dutch died, the papers say.
I learned later,
Returning to the city where he taught me
How to listen,
Help build up another's ego
By digging into my own;
How to speak
When a moment presses with all its might
On ears kept warm by the old pump
Whose workings he knew so well—
The years at the General with bodies
Before the mind made its summons.
All morning with rich analysands,
All afternoon with poor drunks
Who came to a clinic he ran.
We ran, too—eager for his "pearls."
(I started hearing the word in medical school;
I remembered how easily my mother wore them,
How hard they came to us.)

For him psychoanalysis was not the high of heady abstractions;
Rather, to keep steady,
Keep trucking
Through the fog, the crooked paths
Which lead to walls the ancient Chinese would admire—
Until a doctor's words seem late,
Already heard by the patient.
He taught that a mirror
Need not be a fawning or dread double
But, when held at the right angle

To the sun of alert study,
A means of exposure and cautery:
"Warm things up," he once said,
"Then be prepared to take the heat."

Late in life he kept the fires going.
A wise beauty lasted
Until the very end,
So they said who had gotten in dutch,
Who had gone to see Dutch,
Who loved him as a Dutch uncle
As well as a savvy alienist,
Never a stranger to those he "saw"
In ways that helped them see.

GREAT BLANK

Black all over,
The night ignores the stars.
Someone denied us light.
The moon is our feeble sun—
Watches our sleep,
While our heads hunch or hop about.
Have you really looked?
Close and lock your eyes—
The great blank you draw.
The lids will blow
Unless we keep the key turned,
Night capturing day.
The world watches,
Won't wish us well,
Whispers the prayer of a cloudless noon:
There, but for God's grace . . .
And hearing, we hold on.

GOSSIP

Is the invasion
Of undefended territory
By neighbors
Who lust for words
To kill someone, somewhere
(Smiling—a slip of the face);
Who lust for bad news
To have for a feast;
Who can't sleep at night
Without the consoling dream
Of *Fama est*
To remind them
Of lineage and time,
The eastward shadow
Which no sun outside the garden
Has ever dispatched.

Meeting Worlds

PERPENDICULAR

Parallel to each other,
They stare into the mist.
They march and sing to Heaven,
Wipe their smarting eyes of memory's tears.
Never fear a filthy Fenian;
The father's words matched, though:
Pulverize the Prods—
Pride pushing pursed lips.
"A big word,"
The Papist child exults,
Repeats: "Pulverize them."
But the urgent why's return:
"Tell me, ma, what Jesus did,
To make everyone hate everyone."
For His sake is always the answer:
It started on the Cross,
The lad learns, and does the drawing:
Lots of red perpendicular lines,
A shopping bag boast—
"Sale, Everything Must Go."

WELCOME TO MANAGUA

Lenin's chin sweats—
The wires love their sleep:
Somoza's gift of relaxed incompetence.
The *comandante* grants us an audience;
The man who mastered miles of jungle
Screams in the hot air like a baby gasping
For milk he can't have, tells of desire—
A new slavery: "I need air coolers
Much more than cigarettes."
Welcome, answer the ghosts of Managua's hills,
Where ballroom dancing once scorned the seasons,
Where armpits now can't hide the truth:
"People up there had airline schedules
On the table nearest the door."

In the big room the master tosses his remarks,
Eyes up and down the *norteamericanos*.
We wait for English to become
Spanish to become English, one time-out,
Then another: the button summons her
And the wares she offers,
Cookies coffee cream, but no sugar.
He smiles, a confident host,
Waits for swallows, offers more
Food for thought: history's dialectic.
Welcome to a new world,
The two boys hear,
Checking with their father's eyes immediately,
Only to find them hiding in a faint smile;
Irony, detachment, cynicism—

The sins of omission.
Then, more cookies, coffee—the spell of her smiling kindness.

With the fourth coffee, and crumbs
All over, the boy squirms,
New energy lights his mind, moves his tongue.
"Why doesn't he speak to her?"
But a question is a dodge—feinting with a boxer
Who keeps coming back, history at his fingers.
Alright, then, in English:
"You've not once said please or thank you to her,
Not once even looked at her."
The father squirms in his cautionary sweat.
When will the young master the psychology of adjustment?
Up the tower of Babel, and down;
The big shot welcomes the challenge,
Tells the man his child is smart!
He, too, will inherit the future—
The gringo boy who heard the promises,
Saw the lies, broke a mirror in the room
Upstairs, where they say a revolution is trying to stay alive.

APART

Steps across our land,
Their land, the veld;
The view is purple haze at noon
The smell of our black flesh
Fills their Dutch ovens:
A holiday present—
Their roasted new laws,
The Dispensation they use
To slam the door for good
Under the nod of their God.
The key is in their old wagon,
Where they forgot their nightmares,
Locked us in their eyes forever:
Apart from their ivory soul.

THE CAMERA'S MAGIC
To A.H.

Near Noorvik, a tangent to a cold Circle,
The children wave at the black eye,
Wonder about the hanky-panky—
What happens behind the glass.
A grandfather remembers a radio—
Its small people, chattering away
At anyone's call,
Even a tundra boy's.
Now visitors are working again
To tell by show,
To make of all words
What a villager's teacher said:
Words, words, words—
Nodding two continents east,
Thinking centuries backward,
Hoping that space and time
Would huddle that day
For the sake of the future.

"When I see a snap of myself,
I want to look and be quiet."
In the eighth year of her visit
To a community of a hundred
On the edge of a white eternity
Her eyes got the picture
Before she offered the lesson:
"Here, you should watch first;
The sound comes later,"
She told the talkative visitors
While her own lenses focused on debris,
Its silent move across
The tundra's white nowhere—
Until, soon, the wind's uproar.

In the fall of 1960, Ruby Bridges, age six, made a beginning of racial integration in New Orleans by attending the first grade of the Frantz School. The result: a total boycott of that school by white families, and daily mobs that heckled Ruby mercilessly as, escorted by armed federal marshals, she entered or left the building. At the time, I was in charge of the neuropsychiatric section of an Air Force hospital in nearby Mississippi, sent there under the doctor's draft law, now a thing of the past, which required two years of medical duty in the military for all young physicians. I was also seeing a psychoanalyst in New Orleans—part of my training in psychoanalytic child psychiatry. One day I stumbled into the mob scene Ruby had to experience in order to get her lonely education—and soon enough, I would be trying to meet her. For years thereafter, she became an important teacher for my wife and me.

RUBY

You have never reminded me
To ask myself
Where I'd be now
Were you not where you were:
Before those mobs,

Entering that school
To learn alone America's history—
Hearing the shouts, the swears,
Praying rock hard:
Jesus will forgive,
Even those who wanted to kill you.
On my way to the prone position,
The final passage for my kind,
I saw you, and later heard of you—
"A conflict to try to resolve":
To be with you—
Or not to be anywhere near you.
One question a kindly doctor
Sitting way out of sight
But working to hear
Answered by not answering:
"I don't know what to say,"
Thereby giving permission
To find out what *you* had to say,
A job that became a rescue,
Mine by you,
Though, it did take you time:
The "resistance" we doctors
Are heard to mention—
Always when talking of others.

Her words arrived out of God's permission
(Alright, credit Nature):
The brain humming in our way—
The ones whose thing
It is to sing.
But Ruby was not all ears,
Looked long and hard,
Reached with fingers
Before counting them,
Held the crayon like a rod
Meant to divine the eye's sweep—
That now and then cat,
That broom sweeping away time:
A mother's picture to a mother,
Grass with its dandelion jewelry,
Or the dream: African animals
Gobbling yellow candy, while the safari leader,
A precise linguist, frets,
Grabs at some book of origins.
The child knows her continent,
Colors brown the fall meadow grass
Until the red thumb tires,
The green voice asserts its future,
Offers its small surprise,
The sound of words—a shy apology:
"I like drawing pictures
Better than talking about what I see."
The quick smile of afterward recognition
Tells of irony's victory,
But the eyes do not surrender;
They move back to the pictures,
Live off them.

Ruby

Whites had all their fingers;
"I forget mine," Ruby noticed—
But went no further:
The silence of a shy smile.
Brown is not orange—
A long-ago glimmer of melancholy savvy
Now the stuff of every step
Past their daily howl.

"I like red and black together"
(A whispered hope?),
Spoken while making her dress.
"I don't know whether
To use orange or yellow"
(How to take their exact measure?),
Wondered while making his hair—
Then abruptly the brown barrier:
The division of grass separately done;
Her final stroke;
Her sad, reluctant bow to segregation;
Her line of thought;
A line in her poem's progress;
Her step inward:
"That's how it is
For poor us—
And I gave him ears,
So he could hear the hollering,
The swears they say
(I try not to listen;
I sometimes try forgetting I have ears)."

Ruby exhausted brown crayons first—
Signatures for years of drawings.
She forgot a foot now and then:
Wholeness a search not an inheritance.
The yellow suns wear smiles
Even when clouds assailed the sky
With pencil lines of a "reality principle."
The blues of a pointed rain
Knowing its proper direction.
The school took its color from her,
A singular presence of integration.
("They did this 'nigger thing' to us out of the blue,
Just sent her in, dammit.")
The other world assumed its brightness:
Orange covers bodies,
Green, the ground,
Yellow and red a promise
On the other side of her hell.
Suddenly, a line of blue, then another:
A mob's cover,
The halo they sought,
Them become a diminutive threesome.
Pausing, a hard look upward:
"I made them smaller because it would be
Nice if they'd get fewer.
I don't know why the blue is there;
Maybe it fell from the sky!"
Later, an *explication de texte*—
Her Express speeds by Sociology
Passes (surpasses) Psychology:
"The crayons have their colors,

I try to use them right;
Momma, she'll say
You've got to figure out
What the score is."

Concrete Christ is trying to be a bird
Over the city, but He is
Fastened to the mountain.
Why does He come to me at night
While all day I cough and beg?
I hate His concrete. Does He?
They have got Him where they want Him—
No loaves for our bellies.
I know the ones who do tricks
But He smiled and touched them.
(Where? I wonder sometimes.
What did He do with His sex?)
Here above Copacabana the sun beats us up,
The wind is afraid to come near,
But they wear their furs evenings,
Get hot and fingers glitter,
Then their long time with it,
Their coffee at noon—
I know their habits.
Up the hill the tree crouching, whipped by time,
While the boy dares his kite
To take him over the city.

He will break out, the nun said.
No statue can hold Him forever,
My daughter told the mirror,
Her eyes seeing all the bills her body earned.
I remembered the Sister,
A bride of God, I heard someone say.
Sundays they cover themselves well,
The Ipanema big swallow Him,

Drink Him up, followed by brunch,
But not a crack in His cage on the hill.
I hear my daughter counting *norteamericano* paper,
Singing her tune: tomorrow will be the last supper.
No more tomorrows, only pie in the sky—
Until all of us, called home, will laugh
Looking at the Man on the mountain:
The eagle they turned into a parrot,
The lightning they grounded, and still gloat.

The devil rules those streets
We all know. Everyone there
Belongs to him; he is a sly one,
Owned by the Pope, my father insists.
Worse than the Pope, my father told me
The day he pushed me on the swing
While looking at each car that came.
God lost that day! I was going up—
"No" I heard, and down on the ground
We heard the pops, and father prayed to our God.
Her cry swooped upon the street.
Her father became an accident the Pope's boys made.
"When does the voice stop, after death?"
The child keeps asking, until her voice, too,
Must be stilled, through scones and jam from Spain,
Where the Pope's boys harvest oranges,
Pray the Lord will spare them a drought.
The girl thinks of the devil:
"Will he leave Belfast for good one rainy morning,
Tired of all he has to do?"
Stay away,
She whispers to him on her knees in church—
Spots the stain of marmalade on her dress,
Forgets him, prays for the resurrection:
A swath of undefiled cotton, sweet to all eyes.

THE DEVIL II

They are the bosses of Belfast
Riding herd in their black vans,
Which pick up our men beaten and dead,
Dumped later behind their walls.
Lad, he called me, a Police Prod;
He put his stick to my chin,
Pushed my head back to choking surrender.

It's no use fighting them
My father told me on the last day he had:
"Before God made the decision,
The devil got him,
But now God holds him forever."
My father worked all night—
The filth of the Prod shifts;
They made him beg to pick up after them.
The January sun tried to warm us that day,
Failed and turned bright red
In shame and anger at teatime,
Then fell again into God's throat.
He tossed the works at us that night,
The crown jewels scattered everywhere above,
Only we were all blinded
By the holy water of our eyes:
I hate our Church.
My father was a Catholic who fought
Not for the priests but for the people.
We're poor enough here
To save the Pope from Satan,
Who is Prince Consort
For all who pray with Paisley,
Lord pity them.

THE SANDINISTAS WIN

The drums of Managua's latest earthquake
Quickly fell still—only a moment's warning.
People avoid the old holes still in the ground.
But the *comandantes* look upward,
Plan to shake the nation's tree free:
No pasarán, voices tell the world,
While some, awake at night,
Hear the same old noises—
Soldiers guarding Power.
A north wind turns the green uniformed young gray,
Scatters red signs on the streets.
"We will be rid of Dior and Chanel,"
The poor hear,
Scratching their heads,
Watching their sons become Sandinistas.

Take Jesus back from those priests
Whose hearts no longer bleed or beat
The strange music of old Galilee,
Where the Rabbi touched whores,
Slept who knows where,
The Holiday Inns all occupied,
The Ritz full of an empire's
Black ties and dresses for show
At galleries where taste governs—
Another expensive freedom dear to those expansive souls.
He was headed for no big places
He told us in His madness before
The history of the world demanded
An end to the chapter of a visit from the blue.

A boy talks with the *yanqui* doctor:
The smile of memory's loss—
The father touched a mine,
Climbing a monument of Somoza's shame,
Holding in his heart a child's picture.
Now the peasants hear the news:
You are free to see paintings,
Make your own,
Rise to the hills where
The earth did not dare tremble,
Nor children beg their meals outside home.
Soon our muscles will level
The shacks of brute flesh.

The leader's lips move,
Make their point
To the fleeing deaf.
But for all of you, here,
Who remain and remain in history,
Remember: pray when the leader says
Now is the time to rally
Round ancient glory—
Hope the Lamb
Will be dished out
For those who missed the Miami auctioneer's
Call to bargaining order.

LA FRONTERA

An innocent river made guilty,
A culprit by history's doings—
Crimes for those who want in
But are not wanted in.
Still, life is the chase, and so
They run, play hide and seek,
Crawl a lot, as befits underdogs.

The giant has his guard up,
Uses all the new devices,
Says *basta*, worries about
Entries, invasions that will
Contaminate the body politic,
Tries quarantines, scolds and threatens—
A radical approach.
But we hear only our stomachs,
The growl of our need.
We keep creeping to disappear—
To escape history and beat geography.
We have no place to go but up—
Across *la frontera*.

On certain nights, when the moon has left—
No game of show and tell—
The *humildes* do their snake act,
Pupils ready to see the worst,
Learn the end
Before any beginning will ever be.
Back to *la revolución*, the one that stretched
So far it snapped in our faces,
Leaving us in this valley of Spanish dolls,
Crawling to cross
A river that left us behind.

A WIFE, A DIXIE PARTNER
To J.H.C.

She watched as the black child's stare
Sent me running to the familiar,
The wordy litany she'd always called,
Frowning: "Shrink mumbo jumbo."
Her smile and plain talk
Became a sanctuary for those southern boys and girls,
For the doctor who needed
(To twist Fromm's phrase around)
The freedom to escape—
The calculations of professional convention
In a job once thought to be—
Sad, another secular fall—
Spying for the sake of
Good clean anger against
All the smug and phony enemies.

She knew why she left Ohio,
For a school she made
Her own "wonderful town":
A Rosalind ready to redeem
At least one troubled mind
All too sure of its future—
Those cubicles in a mental monastery
At the foot of a doctors' street where
"Wonderful feeling" was sung
By those who dreamed
Of changing into another person.
She had turned her back on all of it—
The speculations of the culture brokers,
The heads touching the stars,
Sure of their metamorphosis,

The cards in gravure,
The spilt high teas,
Waking the last hopes of lawns
Already paled down,
The sherry, as dry as the throats
Taking it, giving right back—
Salon repartee in a season without rain.

Down yonder in the old port,
Sweet night saxophones never silenced,
Louie the king forever,
Ruby slept, awaiting the stage,
Ready to pity people
Ready to kill her;
And a teacher took her husband's hand,
Pulled him into an American scene,
Urged sense and the senses on someone
Whose hearing wasn't quite what he thought,
Whose eyes needed the boost of
Dixie's new lady.

A CAMBRIDGE LIFE

Seized by neural fevers,
The sun far elsewhere,
The moon not yet born,
The heart in lowest gear—though
Suddenly the brain not idling at all,
She goes on her crooked walk
Through the history of abuse:
All the years of names called,
The leers and the punches,
The smell of fired bullets,
The smile suffering can give to life.

She could never forget the teasing,
The childhood of whiskey,
The older boys she learned to hate.
Her son learned not to hate back—
Except in long silences.
The husband followed, broken at last.
With their separate deaths she ruled
The memories of certain survivors,
Her low sweet voice a warning
The oldest granddaughter knew so well;
Walked off the terror on many streets,
Surrendered fitfully for money's sake
To the old one's summer call to the sea.

Her secret madness was the squaw's revenge:
Let the big-shot men sail to the islands,
Dig clams with their long muddy limbs;
I am the psychologist, she let everyone know,
Who visited doctors before the others,

Who recalls nightmares of ruined play,
And a family turned to sticks and stones.

At Christmas she offers tidy presents,
Pushed in pretense, and received alright:
The bitter decoys of a wan widow
Whose long night of restive bluff
Soon gives way to another morning's cold tea kettle.

On the Day Jesus Christ Was Born

CONCORD CHRISTMAS

Surrendering to the thick cover of snow,
The early cold of a winter not yet fully born,
The raccoon lumbers toward the porch,
Daring those who own Sierra Club calendars
To make any kind of refusal.
The tail trips an alarm,
Fires electricity all over.
Did not curiosity kill the cat?
But the raccoon has made its decision—
Aware of all options,
As they proclaim in the White House,
Where in a 1986 winter a chief is dozing,
While flunkies try to plant wires,
Pull strings,
So that everyone will remember
To let the eye's mist,
The music of hailing rule the day.

Sated on charity meant for the winged homeless
("There are no homeless in this town,"
A peacock, who admitted he couldn't fly, remarked)
The raccoon lumbers away,
His ambling laziness a taunt,
His dragging tail a nose lifted to them
Who watch in their light.
Then, all switches *go,*
They summon a shelf of books,
Stop at R, at embryology, histology, neurobiology,
At evolutionary genetics,
Cross-species epistemology—
A reminder that words preceded things.

Raccoons will help us optimists be free:
The raccoon as the proper study of mankind—
Even as popes offer wisdom outside the Vatican.

With all quiet now on the porch front
Concord can come to the town.
Blackness is no longer nearby life.
The children can be fed reindeer,
Followed by that old fat bearded one
Whose denial of his stinginess is obvious
To those who read the Living pages,
And know what the mind is—
The latest place of Dr. Westheimer's worship.
Phooey on her, I think,
But she has "new ideas," *People* says:
What Mr. and Mrs. Claus do
Or should do (the moralist as sexualist)
All those nights before the big one.
We have nothing to fear but fear itself
We hurry to tell a child
Who claims to see reindeer crossing the sky in fullest day.
Soon, when tall enough to press buttons,
Old enough to read print,
He'll be ready to own this century's illusions.

A CHRISTMAS WITHOUT MOTHER AND DAD

The unconscious is timeless she once whispered,
The great man's daughter, herself a large soul.
But only the nightmares at fifty-five
Recalled her words—the return of the repressed,
As we are wont to say in our slight
Hint of the poetry the founding father
Took for granted: Oedipus was not
Born to a social scientist writing a textbook.
To be orphaned at an age some retire
Is to become a child once more,
At the mercy of everything children shrewdly sense—
Then smile watching a parent's "maturity."
Lord, when will we grow up enough
To talk as once we did when boys and girls?

In the dark Santa's red leaves the sleigh,
Speeds an anxious descent,
Mindful of "object-relations,"
Falls upon Dad's maroon Pontiac,
One of the last before Pearl Harbor
Put an end to onyx push button radios
Sounding off as we punched wildly,
Obliging, never protesting,
Though Mother was someone who asked
Mercy for one and all,
Including that radio, whose Eroica she told us
Would prevail, if only we flexed our knees,
Said the words she seemed to know offhand,
Yet spoke with tears we noticed—
Her Iowa cheer
Frightened by Tojo to the west,

The shrieking guttural voice eastward:
God, how can this be?
Dad answered. His hard science
Softened to include the head's hardware.
He sat in the car, his knees bent sharp,
Shunning the floor: *Homo erectus.*
He had given us erector sets, told us
Better Living through Chemistry—
Not only a Delaware motto.
We picked from the menu of his books,
One dish consumed, another meal awaiting;
He shared his vitamins and minerals with us:
"A temporary aberration"—because Milton
Told him as a boy in England that truth will out,
And Orwell, his hero well before others
Knew to follow, had not lost nerve—
Wartime remarks meant to sweeten tea, butter scones.
Only afterward was there a blink:
The white flags bringing a cold war;
The pictures of camps on a library wall
Falling down upon him
Until tears made him
Talk of an allergy.
The science of crematoria
Was not in the M.I.T. curriculum.
Nor would any of Santa Claus' postwar presents
Bring a smile to him, as he kept eating books,
Complaining of a vast indigestion—
The ailments of his century:
Born 1900

"Under Victoria," he would say—
While she cackled for us as we viewed her.

In the end mother found peace in Tolstoy,
Despite her own night cries,
Her eyes wet with Anna's tears,
Her heart beating
To all the bands crossing Europe long ago;
While Dad, on snowy days, with no one seeing
Slipped into a church
To sit, not kneel,
To pray for his grandsons, whose strength is part his:
On behalf of the third millennium,
A few less victories, please,
For the dark angel dispatched our way
In the time before time.

CHRISTMAS IN THE YARD

No communion in the church;
This president has better things to do
While others crawl to Washington.
Mr. Taft's girth was substantial,
But the higher latitude of Cambridge
Will forever be consequential—
Thoughts that matter.
Senior students stare upward of mud,
Look to the lawns of spring's big outdoor theater,
Visit stacks of a library where
Chlorophyll's secrets are among
Billions kept under one Yankee trust
Or another, all watched
By hawks who saw the Red Sox
Down there someplace lose—
But crimson is another color entirely.

A week later Santa Claus shudders
Riding over those cold empty buildings.
His luck is considerable.
A few weeks earlier he'd have been
Brought down cold to face
Those thousands of savvy youths
(Not to mention their nimble mentors)
Who know their numbers and letters,
Know the lessons of Weber and Freud,
Know a consummate, confident, conclusive dance:
A stately waltz, it goes like *this*, like *that*.
So long Santa, try your song,
Your tap dance elsewhere—
Across railroad tracks that circle our yard:
Miles and miles of separation from
The core of a city called Cambridge.

A ROOMING-HOUSE CHRISTMAS

I remember a woman of some gentility, who took in boarders because she was lonely. Her own life had disappointed her; she needed other lives nearby, but she paid them little heed. She was lost in herself.—William Carlos Williams

Where is the view, the long view?
Where is all the snow put now?
What about the kitchen knives left carelessly
In the house's backyard?
She looked out the window,
Could not bear to see a lone blackbird
Picking away at nothing;
But it would not
Come inside, she knew,
To help with those stuffed closets.
She had tried to make the rooms a respectable place.
The doctors had told her about tourniquets;
She had rushed to both of her men,
Hoping to stop their bleeding—
Which made for messy memories
Years after therapy.
In the December morning she continued the mourning,
Cutting Vienna coffee-cake—the gin hidden from view;
The grandchildren must hear only soft whispers—
Her stray-dog psychology phrases.
But Christmas is a Mother and Son day;
She kept wondering about the biology of madness,
Hoping an errant gene would save her
From her own sidelong glances—
The weird silences of the son,
The husband's loss of direction as his life approached the
    harbor.
He wanted for years to dive into the black water;
One day his heart broke as he dreamed of sailing free,
Leaving her with the messy tack—
He who had always been so tidy.

Teasing was her game,
So in tears she told her doctor—
A red-haired cat who lived not quite nine lives.
She dreamed of clawing away at her accusers' heads,
Who dared speak when she pouted,
Or (major signal) turned her gaze elsewhere.
Once the cat scurried for food,
Lunged at a doctor,
Swallowed his dog, but woke her up.
She craved the bottle without the pretense of a glass—
To bottle her own worst demon:
Alone before her mirror's judgment.
Maybe someone's funeral will help, or a musical instrument.
Maybe a volunteer is needed—
To stop the killing, by hand or by bomb.
But what of words?
Maybe Shakespeare will offer cheerful company,
Help her with her midwinter's dream:
That all will be well at the end,
However many fallen heads.
Maybe the baby Jesus gives us a second chance,
But don't you bet on it, she told herself
As she threw the presents at a daughter's door,
Hoping in the car a country drive
Would bring some seasonal peace:
Those kitchen knives out of sight, out of mind.

VIETNAM IN BOSTON, CHRISTMAS

They put up the feeder for the birds,
Full of suet, seeds—their sympathy;
But hungry in a white birthday season,
We kept out of sight,
Worried, maybe, by their big birds
Flying at heights only the grounded can reach,
With their always busy genes
Making one point after another.

The children asked about distances,
Searched faces for flying time,
Remembered all the stories the elders
Said and said, until the shades of
Ancestors enveloped them,
Proving the old piety that
Nature can outlast the worst contrivances—
Until its moment comes.

If birds fly safely through U.S. air,
And U.S. air drops no bombs,
Then *why*, the children ask.
Stop why's, the mother insists.
We are a polite, obedient people,
But in America all children
Become Americans fast;
Everything here goes fast.

They ask another why, I hold
My breath until my chest says
No longer, and when it moves in
I speak out; I say, listen,

You, far away over there is not here.
I say, from air came death,
All the time came whining death.
No holiday stopped death dropping,
Death busy with its visits
Until nothing left to visit;
We all gone
One way or the other.
Birds were first to go.

Here birds come nonstop;
They bring sleep,
Stop pain at top of the head
Better than anyone's acupuncture,
Or your extra-strengths,
Which we now know so well.
Here it is quiet in the middle of night,
Quiet when sun arrives to get busy,
Quiet when sun says so long,
Quiet when head crashes pillow—
When I always say thanks to You,
Wherever You're staying these days.

THINKING OF HOPPER ON A
DIXIE CHRISTMAS

Nighthawks here also fly,
Eye up high the Dixie dew
On beer cans held by all
The talkers who chain-smoke,
Trash their lives with but's.
We had a moment with the December stars;
They fell on Alabama near Zelda's nursery,
Where she learned so early
The necessity of separation—
North to places, but not Nyack,
Where the boy Edward, no philosopher,
Already pictured those "vacant inter-stellar spaces"
Down home on the Hudson.
A southern lady of gumption,
She would not have shunned the El,
Fled a downtown diner. Everything was game.
She piled hope upon hope,
But one day the melancholy descent.
Someone else would find
The soul's truth
On city roofs, in a hotel room
Sitting on the bed, her suitcases packed,
Ready to return, maybe southward—
Wearing the hat on that bookcase:
A painter's nod to the street
We leave, undressed, alone
On our frequent one-night stays.

CHRISTMAS, NEW MEXICO, 1973

The snow warms to a sun
With no place to hide today,
The slush a joke to our horses,
Who draw their hooves
As children once did with chalk
On the streets of distant cities:
Here is where we stand.
Does God get impatient,
Draw his own lines, the stars,
Signals of His turf, His intentions?

In Las Trampas I climbed a trail, then a tree—
A big aspen, yet quickly vulnerable,
Its branches, undecided, tremble:
To put up with him
Or let him go?
It can be painful to be a good host,
But it hurts to say no.
Kept aloft, I looked at the village,
My camera copying me.
A cluster of old adobe houses
Lined up like tired veterans—
All the give and take
In many a monopoly game:
The making of Americans.
Domingo's house, biggest of all,
Showed bright pink in the noon light
Like a hotel for Park Place or Boardwalk.

I notice dead aspen leaves,
Once part of a spring's green,

An autumn's red and yellow blanket.
Their watch is long over,
Yet they won't go the way of forgotten memories,
Prefer to gaze at a nearby wonder:
Fresh green hay on the new snow;
Four black and white cows grazing casually,
As if owners of a time-machine
They'd shifted into reverse;
One white horse chewing, tail swishing;
Five chickens pecking away
(No partridge, no pear tree),
All needing no holiday salutations,
No *merry*, no *peace*,
Only the munching and gobbling of
Live and Let Live,
Seen by *una anciana*, I notice,
Her snowshoes parked at the road's edge.
She points proudly—to no one, it seems,
Until she puts the palms of her hands together,
Looks upward, smiles at the sun's touch,
Keeps her lips moving.

CHRISTMAS, BELFAST

We have a Catholic mum and a Protestant mum here [in Belfast], and
they want us all to make friends for Christmas. I think they'll be disappointed!
—a nine-year-old Belfast girl whose parents dared "intermarry"

Waterford crystal smuggled from the Republic into Paisley's
    turf,
An excuse for the children to know beauty,
Stare into the infinity of a ball,
See, maybe, the light of God's birth
Still trying to hit our eyes,
Give us sight beyond our here.
"Ma, why did you sit with a Pape woman?"
"Ma, why did you smile at that Prod lady?"
But no matter the refrains,
The two sat in one church, another:
Visitors following refractions through corridors of time,
Hoping the bleeding heart
(The one framed by the nuns)
Will stop altogether—
Become the new beat of an island's infant life.

They held hands, two mothers ready to toss
Paisley and the Pope to the wolves of Belfast,
Where blood is thicker than the mud,
The slime of the Irish Sea,
Where the traffic of hate, back and forth, began,
No matter His trip—
So important, the preachers say, to all of us.
"If we can come together on Christmas
Others can follow"—the old faith in leadership:
Come ye, follow me.
But soon a million roads,
Each got with bows and arrows, guns, planes:
The ascent of man it is called—
Our killing tools.

They spoke their dreams at noon,
The light of Norway passing them,
Trying for Greenland before a quick death.
If only they both could deliver on His birthday
A pair of celebrations, and all Ulster
Would take notice—
Leave bad words at the door,
The kitchen warm with their cooking.

CHRISTMAS, RIO DE JANEIRO

I will tell you, Doctor, I sleep with those men to get their money.
Otherwise my children would starve. Afterward, I give to the Church.
I am money's mistress. I feel no shame.

Sweat on the nun's upper lip;
She lowers her head as she passes
Bread I stole: loaves and loaves,
Dates and nuts, the fruits of a life
Picked after the customers doze their sated dreams.
Don't give them your love,
You'll be clean: the old grandma's advice.
She should know! I heard
Her shout to God:
"Our family's luck—a one and only star born."
I use my wits,
Go with what I have,
God's gifts to me.
I pray for blood—
Each month's visit a clean blessing:
Work, the light of the world,
As Jesus the man knew
When He did not turn from certain women.

In the hotels I am of this world—
Knuckles skimming silk,
The gold blinding, yet I see them,
Hear their bargaining sounds
All through the fast night:
I travel a million miles a minute.
Life is a breeze, the flower knows,
Looking at the bent tree—
So much action, so little time.

Come all ye, make a visit to Me.
Don't fear the Copacabana sand,

The big soft pillows on the wicker chairs,
The Benz bringing you near the cypresses,
Where in the morning the women mourn,
Gratefully remember:
The young carpenter
Who loved them,
No matter what.

CHRISTMAS, MANAGUA, 1986

Midnight brings the chickens down
Her life, their perch. They flutter,
Land in her mind and peck
Their way to her restless limbs, the fingers
Ready to pluck, the arms to carry,
The legs running from the night's stillness,
The long empty hours, and then, with luck, the sight:
Old feathers, lard, flour, and always,
Slogans, a diet rich in abstractions.

The toes curl as the chickens kick up dust;
A rooster boasts its sovereignty
While the loudspeaker brings us a boss,
Boss of bosses, eyes behind New York shades,
Looking always to the future.
Up a hill where the future took over
Houses left by the past, chickens roam—
Everywhere ready to sacrifice themselves
Por la revolución, the cry of geese, too:
Flying that old path of plunder,
The North-South axis of history's wheel.
She rolls as the rooster hits upon the Gucci shoes;
They never left those floors of parquetry,
The mainstay of all rule.
The eyes open to the ordinary darkness at midnight.
Since Koestler we have progressed twelve hours,
Lost even the hope of his irony.
We are left with shops whose trays bear no burden,
Left with young men hiding from guns,
Left with young men running to guns,

Left with priests in search of the right pecking order:
"I was so empty in the belly last night
I dreamed we all had become chickens—
But we had nothing to eat.
My daughter had become a chicken like me.
She asked if chickens eat chickens.
It was then I flew to my bed.
Later, I woke up hungry."

CHRISTMAS, PRETORIA

When will your Washington stop pushing us to the edge? When will your Washington try to understand us?—An Afrikaner youth of fifteen

In Holland it was water everywhere, here native flesh—
The symmetry: flesh *is* water.
Further: ocean dark water and dark flesh;
But stop your generalizations—you
Who claim to afford them in an America
Where reservations were built
Because of a conqueror's reservations.
We are tired of the frightened eyes
Upon us from places called abroad.
Native eyes? No problem;
They look inward, and what they see is
Their business. But *you*—
Our voices rise to you, our eyes
Will fight you with the books
We read of "The States"—
What happened and still happens;
Our pink flesh reddens.
Suicide is *your* game.
We did not come here,
Fight to stay here,
With Hamlet in mind, or Camus:
You are the strangers—
All that confusion of pro and con,
All that mention of shadows and ghosts,
Of "problems" and "transitions" ahead—
Angelic angst in well-appointed parlors.

For Christ's sake, we know it is His birthday!
"Your endless holier-than-thou sermons!"
We'll recognize Him today
For what He has always been—

70

All those centuries, when (let's face it)
We crossed the continents to conquer
For Him, for us as His followers,
With no one writing editorials,
Taking those mournful pointing pictures.
Who said time brings progress?
Our jails can accommodate time;
Our vision is the sight of a steady rifle.

The blur is not ours.
It is foes from afar
Who are nearsighted,
Blind to what is at stake:
A Christmas eve that demands its tomorrow.
In America the winter solstice has come;
Here it is summer—though if
Snow White were to visit us
We would never let her melt.

CHRISTMAS, SOWETO

*It is heartbreaking to see them, lines and lines of them, our blacks,
going to our white homes. I have watched and wondered what they
think as they come to care for us. —Alan Paton*

A thick coal mist fights Jo'berg's sun;
The rays press, penetrate, scatter along
The brown clay paths, always ready to accept the feet
Which earlier started the morning trek
Toward the distant lights of stores and offices,
While dreams glowed with their testimony
Of "wish fulfillment" hours before the sales
Would do the bidding of a "collective unconscious."
The little girl wants to know where her mother goes,
Gets told "there, to them,"
Looks up at the night,
Surrenders her mother to it, and then herself,
Pictures a castle with a gate,
Many going in,
Frisked then hurried along
To floors that need scrubbing,
Clothes that need collecting, carrying—
To be put through their baptism (so many times)
Returned for the display of *his, hers*.
"The worst is when the girl asks her questions,
Then they take hold of me, sitting on the bus."
The answers try breaking free—but no:
"I hush the child,
I say I pick up after them."
She picks up as she talks—
A day off, at last.
A day unlike the others—
The ironing, dusting, cooking,
The bending and lifting,
The arranging for their arrangements,

The looking straight on—
The blue eyes hitting the black ones directly with directions;
And the other kind of vision:
Slant, sly, sloe-eyed it gets called.
And the hearing: "Don't be dumb,"
They'll tell you when they've slipped,
And want you to take a slide
So they will conquer always, their history,
Which has given us the secret pleasure
Of our single dominance—overhearing.
Their secrets become our stories—
The dust and dirt they forget
To notice when they tell us to work harder,
Clean up our act, their lives.
"I goes back a slump of a person."
But a child's rush gives her one—
Up in the air the girl goes,
Followed by food,
Lots of fries and cola and rice,
The soft bread that pads life a little.
In bed the child's eyes flicker—and out.
But nearby the fires of evening spread
Their many alarms—the *shebeens*, all filled up,
Pour their oil and the whole township
(The word another London export) lives true
To Shakespeare's habit: the rising action
Of flanks and hips, the falling action
As the play of night bows abruptly
To a western silence—
The gavel of their law, their order:

Jet planes cutting through the sky,
Pounding the verdict of unprincipled power.

Later the pilots, notice served,
Will pick up their presents
In those precincts of Pretoria
Where Pilate still sits strong.